LUCCA TRAVEL GUIDE

2024

Your Pocket Guide to Lucca: Discover Hidden Gems, Top Attractions and Culinary Delights in this Enchanting Tuscan Escape

BY

NELSON FELICIA

TABLE OF CONTENT

MY MOST RECENT TRIP TO LUCCA

I recently enjoyed traveling to Lucca, a lovely walled city in Tuscany, Italy. Although the vacation was brief, I packed a lot into it and had a great time.

My first day began with an early afternoon arrival in Lucca, where I checked into my hotel. I then left the house to go sightseeing. The Piazza dell'Anfiteatro, a lovely oval area constructed on the ruins of a Roman amphitheater, was my first destination. I strolled around the plaza taking in the vibrant architecture and bustling atmosphere. I then made a visit at one of the numerous cafes for a coffee and a croissant. I had a coffee break and then went to explore Lucca. Beautiful views of the city and the surrounding countryside were available as I strolled up the top of the city walls. I also went to a few of the several churches in Lucca, including the Duomo di San Martino, the city's cathedral.

I had supper at one of Lucca's numerous top-notch restaurants in the evening. I had a wonderful supper of fish and pasta with tiramisu for dessert. I went for a stroll around the city's historic district after supper since it was so gorgeously lit up at night.

I went to a few of Lucca's museums on my second day there. The National Museum of Palazzo Mansi, which holds a collection of Renaissance and Baroque art, is where I began. The National Museum of Villa Guinigi is a stunning villa with a rooftop garden that provides sweeping views of the city, so I went there next. I grabbed lunch at a little eatery in the city center after my museum tours. Pasta and salad were a simple yet excellent supper for me. I went shopping after lunch and bought some trinkets for my loved ones.

I ate my last meal in Lucca that evening. I visited a spot renowned for serving authentic Tuscan fare. I ate a wonderful supper of grilled meat and veggies and finished it off with panna cotta. I strolled around the city's historic district one final time after supper before returning to my hotel.

Overall, my journey was quick yet pleasant to Lucca. I spent a great time discovering the city's stunning architecture, extensive history, and delectable cuisine. Anyone searching for a lovely and peaceful holiday should go to Lucca, in my opinion.

THE AIM OF THIS GUIDEBOOK

The Lucca Travel Guide goes beyond the bounds of traditional travel companions, aiming to be a conduit for engaging experiences as well as a store of knowledge. My goal in creating this compilation is to reflect the rhythm of Lucca, a city steeped in history and resonant with cultural cadence. My goal is to serve as the compass for the inquisitive and the key to discovering the hidden gems inside the centuries-old walls and cobblestone streets.

This directory is more than just a list of places to see; it's a journey through history and custom. You will explore the maze of Renaissance splendor and medieval charm as you unravel Lucca's tapestry. Each page is a call to explore the piazzas where the rustling of olive leaves and the symphony of tastes in the neighborhood trattorias may be heard.

I shed light on the lesser-known treasures, those whispered secrets only known to the locals, beyond the typical sites. Monuments are just a small part of Lucca's soul; the city also radiates through its bustling marketplaces, friendly locals, and timeless tunes that may be heard in obscure places. This travel guide offers more than simple directions; it also provides a road plan for experiencing Lucca's pulse. I invite travelers to explore the winding lanes with awe, to take in the artwork painted on church ceilings, and to take part in the vibrant celebrations that mark the year.

This book is, in essence, a tribute to Lucca's soul—a remembrance of the city's history, a celebration of its present, and a manual for creating bonds that last long after the trip is over. Discovering Lucca is important, but so is falling in love with it.

CHAPTER ONE

Introduction to Lucca

Overview of Lucca

The city of Lucca, which is steeped in history and is surrounded by the Tuscan countryside, is a tribute to both the tenacity of human creation and the passage of time. This gem of a city, located in the center of Italy, charms tourists with its medieval allure, architectural magnificence, and a rich cultural legacy that reverberates throughout its cobblestone streets.

The city was founded in antiquity, and its foundations may have been built on the remains of ancient Etruscan villages. But Lucca really started to take up during the Roman period, becoming a significant crossroads for trade and commerce. Even though they are undetectable, the city's early significance is nonetheless hinted at by the vestiges of Roman architecture.

The impressively well-preserved medieval walls that enclose Lucca like a protective embrace are what really set the city apart. These powerful defenses, which were first built to protect against outside threats, today provide a charming promenade that welcomes both inhabitants and guests to walk along and take in panoramic views of the city and its surroundings. Walking the walls is like entering a time warp where the present and the past are one.

The center of Lucca, a maze-like maze of winding alleyways and piazzas that emanate a timeless appeal, is nestled inside these ancient defenses. Due to its oval shape, the Piazza dell'Anfiteatro, the area's focal point, harkens back to the spectacles of ancient Rome. Today, it welcomes vivacious markets, colorful events, and laughing echoes that resound against the ancient façade. Beyond its fortifications, the skyline of Lucca is punctuated by the high towers of churches and basilicas, adding to the city's rich architectural tapestry.

With its ornate façade and the spectacular Labyrinth of Lucca set in its floor, the Cathedral of St. Martin, a masterpiece of Pisan Romanesque architecture, attracts attention. Each architectural wonder tells a tale of creative genius and religious fervor, evoking admiration and reflection.

Lucca is more than just a throwback; it is a thriving cultural center that fosters a vibrant artistic culture that expertly combines traditional and modern expression. The city's annual Summer Festival, held inside its ancient walls, turns courtyards and squares into outdoor theaters where audiences may enjoy performances while listening to world-famous artists perform. It's a festival that perfectly captures Lucca's character: an unwavering fusion of history and vitality. Beyond its artistic and architectural gems, Lucca is a foodie's paradise, luring visitors with the delicacies of Tuscany. Trattorias and osterias in the area provide food that honors ancient traditions, where simplicity and complexity coexist and the quality of the ingredients speaks for itself.

Lucca reveals its attractiveness as a romantic destination in the late afternoon when the sun casts a warm glow over the city. Cobblestone alleyways and lit turrets beckon leisurely strolls and inspire introspection among centuries-old trees. In this city, time appears to have stopped, enabling both locals and tourists to appreciate the beauty of the present.

In conclusion, Lucca stands out as a masterpiece in the vast fabric of Italian towns, meticulously woven with threads of culture, history, and classic beauty. The building's walls serve not only as physical limits but also as the custodians of a remarkable heritage, welcoming anyone who enters to take part in its ongoing history.

Lucca History and Background

The picturesque city of Lucca, which is located in Tuscany, Italy, has a rich tapestry of historical importance. There is evidence of a pre-Roman village, and its roots date back to the Etruscans.

15

Lucca changed throughout time, becoming a Roman colony in 180 BC, and its advantageous position aided in its growth. Built during the 16th and 17th centuries, the city's well-preserved medieval walls symbolize Lucca's continuing personality. These walls, which are now a promenade lined with trees, provide sweeping vistas of the city and serve as evidence of Lucca's perseverance throughout history. Within these fortifications, the city's winding alleyways display layers of history, from Renaissance wonders to Romanesque and Gothic grandeur.

Lucca became a thriving commercial hub known for its silk manufacture throughout the Middle Ages. The Guinigi Tower, which is capped with holm oaks, serves as a reminder of the prosperity of the city at the time. Giacomo Puccini, a composer who was born in Lucca in 1858, and other notables were drawn by the city's strong economy, which supported creative and cultural triumphs.

16

In Lucca, an annual opera festival honors Puccini's contributions to the musical world, preserving his legacy. The exquisite 17th-century opera theater in the city, Teatro del Giglio, reverberates with the entrancing tones of Puccini's masterpieces. The Cathedral of Saint Martin and the Church of San Michele in Foro are two stunning examples of religious architecture that dot the landscape of Lucca. The latter illustrates the city's fusion of religious and artistic enthusiasm with its magnificent façade covered with sculptures.

Political upheavals have occurred throughout Lucca's history, including periods of independence, domination by several Italian powers, and even Napoleonic conquest. Every chapter has left a permanent imprint on the city, adding to its unique personality. While incorporating modern aspects, modern Lucca embraces its ancient past. The city's squares, like the Piazza dell'Anfiteatro, bustle with activity as they host markets, celebrations, and events. One of the biggest events of its type in Europe, the annual Lucca Comics & Games convention draws fans from all over the world.

In summary, in a sense, Lucca is a living museum that welcomes tourists to wander through its narrow alleyways and take in the sounds of bygone eras. The vibrancy of current life blends well with the resonance of history in this metropolis.

Geography and Climate

The geography of Lucca is diverse, with a variety of landscapes to explore. The city center is flat, with narrow streets and medieval buildings. The walls of Lucca are a popular tourist attraction, offering stunning views of the city and the surrounding countryside. Outside the walls, the landscape is more rural, with rolling hills, vineyards, and olive groves.

Lucca's climate is Mediterranean, with mild, rainy winters and hot, sunny summers. The average temperature in **January is 4°C (39°F),** and the average temperature in **July is 25°C (77°F).** Rainfall is heaviest in the winter months, and the city experiences occasional thunderstorms in the summer.

Here is a more detailed overview of the geography and climate of Lucca:

Geography:

Lucca's City Center: The city center is located on a flat plain, with narrow streets and medieval buildings. The main square, the Piazza dell'Anfiteatro, is built on the site of a Roman amphitheater. The city also has a number of other important historical sites, including the Duomo di San Martino, the Church of San Michele in Foro, and the Guinigi Tower.

Lucca's Walls: The walls of Lucca are one of the city's most iconic features. The walls were built in the 12th and 13th centuries to protect the city from invaders. Today, the walls are a popular tourist attraction, offering stunning views of the city and the surrounding countryside.

The Serchio River: The Serchio River flows through the city of Lucca. The river is a popular spot for swimming, boating, and fishing.

The Surrounding Hills and Mountains: Lucca is surrounded by hills and mountains, including the Apuan Alps to the north and the Monte Pisano to the south. The hills and mountains offer a variety of hiking and biking trails, as well as stunning views of the city and the countryside.

Climate:

Temperature: Lucca's climate is Mediterranean, with mild, rainy winters and hot, sunny summers. The average temperature in January is **4°C (39°F)**, and the average temperature in July is **25°C (77°F).**

Rainfall: Rainfall is heaviest in the winter months, and the city experiences occasional thunderstorms in the summer. The average annual rainfall in Lucca is **800 millimeters (31 inches)**.

Sunshine: Lucca receives an average of 2,500 hours of sunshine per year. The sunniest months are **June, July, and August.**

Tips for visiting Lucca:

- The best time to visit Lucca is in the **spring or fall.** During these months, the weather is mild and there are fewer tourists than in the summer.
- If you are visiting Lucca during the summer, be sure to stay hydrated and wear sunscreen. The summers in Lucca can be very hot and humid.
- Lucca is a very walkable city. You can easily explore the city center and the walls on

Local Phrases and Greetings in Lucca

In Lucca, a city in Tuscany, Italy, the local language is Italian. Here are some common phrases and greetings in Italian:

1. Hello/Hi - **Ciao**

2. Good morning - **Buongiorno**

3. Good afternoon - **Buon pomeriggio**

4. Good evening - **Buona sera**

5. Good night - **Buona notte**

6. How are you? - **Come stai?** (informal) / **Come sta? (formal)**

7. What's your name? - **Come ti chiami**? (informal) / **Come si chiama**? (formal)

8. My name is... - **Mi chiamo**...

9. Please - **Per favore**

10. Thank you - **Grazie**

11. You're welcome - **Prego**

12. Excuse me / I'm sorry - **Mi scusi** (formal) / **Scusa** (informal)

13. Yes - **Sì**

14. No - **No**

15. Goodbye - **Arrivederci** (formal) / **Addio** (more formal) / **Ciao** (informal)

16. Nice to meet you - **Piacere di conoscerti (informal) / Piacere di conoscerla (formal)**

17. Where is...? - **Dove si trova...?**

18. How much does it cost? - **Quanto costa**?

19. I don't understand - **Non capisco**

20. Can you help me? - **Puoi aiutarmi?**

21. I'm lost - **Mi sono perso/a**

22. Do you speak English? - **Parli inglese?**

23. I love this place - **Amo questo posto**

24. What do you recommend? - **Cosa mi consigli?**

25. I need a doctor - **Ho bisogno di un medico**

26. Where is the bathroom? - **Dove si trova il bagno?**

27. I'm vegetarian - **Sono vegetariano/a**

28. This is delicious - **È delizioso/a**

29. Cheers! (when toasting) - **Salute**!

30. I'm just looking - **Sto solo guardando**

These phrases should come in handy as you navigate through conversations in Lucca. Enjoy your time there!

Population and Ethnics

Italy's Tuscany region is home to the city of Lucca, which has a population of around **90,000**. The city is renowned for both its exquisite Renaissance architecture and its well maintained medieval fortifications. The population of Lucca is similarly varied, with residents from all around Italy and the globe.

Italians (**95%** of the population) make up the majority in Lucca. *The following other ethnic groups are present in the city:*

- African Americans: 2%
- East Europeans: 1%
- African Americans: 1%
- Other: 1%

Morocco is the country with the greatest immigrant population in Lucca, followed by Albania and Romania. Most of the immigrants in Lucca are young people who moved there for employment.

With a median age of **45**, Lucca's population is quite youthful. **40%** of the population in the city holds a university degree. Along with being comparatively wealthy, Lucca has a greater GDP per capita than the national average.

Some of the various ethnic groups that are represented in Lucca's population are those listed below:

1. Italian: The majority of people in Lucca are of Italian descent. While there are individuals here from all around Italy, Tuscans make up the majority.

2. Moroccan: The biggest immigrant group in Lucca is the Moroccan community. A lot of Moroccans have relocated to Lucca to work in agriculture or construction.

3. Albanian: The second-largest immigrant group in Lucca is the Albanian people. Many Albanians have relocated to Lucca in order to work in retail or restaurants.

4. Romanians: The third-largest immigrant group in Lucca is the community of Romanians. Many Romanians have relocated to Lucca to work in the medical or industrial industries.

Lucca's ethnic mix contributes to the city's strength. The many cultures and traditions that are present in the city contribute to the rich cultural life of Lucca. The city's dedication to diversity is also evident in the initiatives and policies it has in place. For instance, the city provides cultural events and language training to aid in the integration of immigrants.

The city of Lucca is friendly to visitors from all walks of life. One of the city's great pleasures is its multicultural populace.

Open time for Lucca

City Walls

Open: 24 hours a day, 7 days a week

Guinigi Tower

- **Open**: Tuesday-Thursday: 9:00am-7:30pm, last admission 6:00pm

- **Wednesday, Friday, Saturday**: 12:00pm-7:30pm, last admission 6:00pm

- **First and third Sunday of the month**: 9:00am-7:30pm, last admission 6:00pm

- **Closed**: Monday, second, fourth, and fifth Sunday of the month, December 25, January 1

Clock Tower

- **Open**: Tuesday-Saturday: 10:00am-1:00pm and 2:00pm-5:00pm

- **Closed**: Sunday, Monday, and holidays

National Museum of Villa Guinigi

- **Open**: Tuesday and Thursday: 9:00am-7:30pm, last admission 6:00pm
- **Wednesday, Friday, and Saturday:** 12:00pm-7:30pm, last admission 6:00pm
- **First and third Sunday of the month:** 9:00am-7:30pm, last admission 6:00pm
- **Closed**: Monday, second, fourth, and fifth Sunday of the month, December 25, January 1

Other Museums

- **Galleria Nazionale di Palazzo Mansi:** Tuesday-Sunday: 10:00am-6:00pm
- **Museo del Fumetto e dell'Immaginario: Tuesday-Sunday: 10:00am-6:00pm**
- **Museo Nazionale della Villa Guinigi**: Tuesday and Thursday: 9:00am-7:30pm, last admission 6:00pm
- **Museo di Palazzo Pfanner**: Tuesday-Sunday: 10:00am-6:00pm

Churches

- Most of the churches in Lucca are open to the public during daylight hours

Shops

- Most shops in Lucca are open from Monday to Saturday, from 9:00am to 1:00pm and 3:00pm to 7:30pm
- Some shops may close for lunch between 1:00 pm and 3:00pm
- On Sundays, most shops are open from 10:00am to 1:00pm

Restaurants

- Most restaurants in Lucca are open for lunch and dinner, seven days a week
- Some restaurants may have shorter opening hours on Mondays

CHAPTER TWO

Planning Your Trip

Best Time to Visit Lucca

Lucca is a popular tourist destination, and it can be quite crowded during the summer months. However, the best time to visit Lucca is during the shoulder seasons of spring (April-June) and fall (September-October).

During the spring and fall, the weather in Lucca is mild and sunny, with average temperatures ranging from **15-25 degrees Celsius**. This is ideal weather for exploring the city on foot or by bike. You can also enjoy leisurely meals outdoors at one of Lucca's many restaurants and cafes. Another advantage of visiting Lucca during the shoulder seasons is that there are fewer tourists. This means that you can more easily get into popular attractions and find accommodation at a reasonable price.

You will also have a more authentic experience of Lucca, as you will be able to interact more with locals.

Here is a more detailed breakdown of the pros and cons of visiting Lucca during each season:

Summer (July-August)

- **Pros**: Long days, warm weather, and many festivals and events.
- **Cons**: Crowded, expensive accommodation, and hot weather (temperatures can reach up to 35 degrees Celsius).

Spring (April-June)

- **Pros**: Mild weather, fewer tourists, and lower accommodation rates.
- **Cons**: Some businesses may be closed or have reduced hours during the low season.

Fall (September-October)

- **Pros**: Mild weather, fewer tourists, and lower accommodation rates.

- **Cons**: Some businesses may be closed or have reduced hours during the low season.

Winter (November-March)

- **Pros**: Very few tourists, lowest accommodation rates, and the opportunity to experience Lucca's Christmas markets.
- **Cons**: Cold weather, short days, and some businesses may be closed or have reduced hours.

Events and festivals

If you are interested in attending a specific event or festival, be sure to check the calendar before booking your trip. Some popular events in Lucca include:

- **Lucca Summer Festival**: A month-long festival of music, theater, and dance (July-August).
- **Lucca Comics & Games:** One of the largest comic book and gaming conventions in Europe (October).

- **Luminaria di Santa Croce**: A religious festival in which the city is lit by thousands of candles (September).

Duration of Stay

Lucca, a lovely city in Tuscany, Italy, draws tourists in with its deep history, magnificent medieval buildings, and easygoing way of life. The amount of depth you desire in an experience will determine how long you should spend in Lucca. The city's well-preserved Renaissance fortifications, the renowned Torre Guinigi with its treetop garden, and the elaborate Cathedral of St. Martin façade may all be seen within a quick **two- to three-day** visit.

However, extending your stay to **five days** gives you the chance to discover Lucca's hidden treasures for a more in-depth experience with its essence. Wander through quaint, cobblestone lanes to find hidden trattorias offering delectable regional fare.

The Piazza dell'Anfiteatro, an elliptical space that pays homage to its Roman amphitheater roots, merits calm days when you may have cappuccino at outdoor cafés and take in the lively ambiance. Going beyond the city limits reveals the Tuscan countryside, which is filled with olive orchards and vineyards. To further your research of the area, think about taking a day excursion to neighboring Florence or Pisa, both of which are accessible by rail.

A week or longer will provide those who want to really immerse themselves in Lucca's culture and community time for unplanned discoveries. Attend community gatherings, converse with local craftspeople, and even enroll in a cooking class to learn the secrets of Tuscan food. Slow travel highlights the subtleties of everyday life and fosters a relationship with the place that goes beyond the norm for tourists.

In essence, the length of time spent in Lucca is a delicate balancing act between a fleeting gaze and a leisurely embrace. Each moment in this Tuscan jewel delivers a look into a bygone age entwined with the warmth of current Italian living, whether it is a quick escape or a prolonged stay.

Budgeting and Costs

Here is a breakdown of spending and budgeting for a visitor to Lucca for the first time:

Accommodation:

- Look for inexpensive hotels or potential Airbnb accommodations.
- Depending on your tastes, plan on spending between **€80** and **€150** each night.

Transportation:

- Consider incorporating flights, trains, and rental automobiles in your mobility budget.

- Include modes of local transportation inside Lucca, such as bicycles or buses.

Food:

- Set aside money for eating out and experiencing the local food.
- Depending on your eating preferences, set a daily budget of between **€20** and **€40**.

Sightseeing and Activities:

- Find out about attractions' admission costs.
- Spend money on things like guided tours and museum visits.

Shopping:

- Set aside money for mementos or distinctive regional goods.
- Depending on your own interests, decide on a suitable purchasing budget.

Emergency Reserve:

- Prepare for unforeseen costs or crises.
- Maintain a reserve of **10–15%** of your overall budget.

Exchange Rates and Charges:

- Think about transaction costs and possible currency conversion rates.
- For better rates and reduced costs, use local ATMs.

Travel Protection:

- Your budget should account for the expense of travel insurance.
- Make sure you have travel cancellation and medical emergency coverage.

Miscellaneous:

- Include ancillary costs like tipping, local SIM cards, and internet fees.

Emergency Fund:

- Keep a little emergency money on hand for unanticipated events or unplanned activities.

Always do your homework and adjust these budgets to suit your interests and manner of travel. Lucca is a wonderful destination, and careful planning of your spending will allow you to enjoy yourself without worrying about money. Travel safely.

Visa and Travel Documents

Whether or not you need a visa to enter Lucca depends on your nationality. Citizens of the European Union (EU), the European Economic Area (EEA), and Switzerland can visit Lucca without a visa for up to **90** days in any **180-day** period. Citizens of most other countries need a visa to visit Lucca. You can apply for an Italian visa at the Italian embassy or consulate in your home country. The visa application process can vary depending on your nationality, so it is important to check with the Italian embassy or consulate in your home country for specific requirements.

Required Documents

The following documents are typically required for an Italian visa application:

- A valid passport
- A completed visa application form
- Two passport-size photos
- Proof of travel insurance
- Proof of accommodation in Italy
- Proof of sufficient funds to support your stay in Italy

Visa Fees

The visa fee for an Italian visa varies depending on your nationality and the type of visa you are applying for. For example, the visa fee for a short-stay tourist visa for citizens of the United States is **$160**.

Processing Time

The processing time for an Italian visa application can vary depending on the Italian embassy or consulate where you apply.

However, it is typically two to four weeks.

Travel Documents

In addition to your visa, you will also need a valid passport to travel to Lucca. Your passport must be valid for at least six months after your date of entry to Italy.

You may also want to consider bringing the following travel documents with you to Lucca:

- A copy of your visa
- A copy of your travel insurance
- A copy of your accommodation reservation
- A copy of your flight itinerary
- A credit or debit card
- A map of Lucca
- A phrasebook or dictionary

Tips for Applying for an Italian Visa

- Apply for your visa well in advance of your trip.
- Make sure that you have all of the required documents.
- Complete the visa application form accurately and completely.
- Be prepared to answer questions about your travel plans.
- If you have any questions about the visa application process, contact the Italian embassy or consulate in your home country.

Packing Essentials

Clothing:

When packing for a trip to Lucca, it is important to consider the climate and the activities you will be doing. In the summer, you will need light, comfortable clothing, such as shorts, T-shirts, and dresses. In the winter, you will need warmer clothing, such as jeans, sweaters, and a coat.

Here is a sample clothing list for a 15-week backpacking trip through Lucca:

- 10 shirts (4-5 T-shirts, 2-3 long-sleeved shirts, 1-2 tank tops)
- 5 pants (2-3 pairs of jeans, 1 pair of shorts, 1 pair of leggings)
- 1 skirt or dress
- 1 hoodie or jacket
- 1 raincoat
- 2 pairs of shoes (1 pair of sneakers, 1 pair of sandals)
- 7 pairs of underwear
- 7 pairs of socks
- 2 bras and sports bras (if applicable)
- 1 swimsuit

If your itinerary includes beaches or pools.
Rain Gear:
- A waterproof jacket or poncho.

Headwear:
- Sun hat or cap for sun protection.

Sunglasses:

- UV protection is essential.

Backpack:

- A sturdy, comfortable backpack with multiple compartments.

Daypack:

- A smaller backpack for day trips and hikes.

Money Belt:

- To keep your valuables secure.

Toiletries:

- Travel-sized Toiletries:
- Toothbrush, toothpaste, shampoo, conditioner, etc.

First Aid Kit:

- Basic medical supplies and any necessary medications.

Sunscreen:

- High SPF for sun protection.

Electronics:

- Adapter for charging your electronic devices.

Power Bank:

- For charging on the go.

Camera:

- Capture memories of your trip.

Documents:

- Passport and Visa, ensure they're valid for the duration of your trip.

Travel Insurance:

- Essential for medical emergencies.

Emergency Contacts:

- Write down important numbers.

Miscellaneous:

- Reusable Water Bottle
- Stay hydrated throughout your journey.

Snacks:

- Non-perishable snacks for energy.

Guidebook/Map:

- Useful for navigation and recommendations.

Travel Pillow:

- For more comfortable rest during transportation.

Activities:

- Hiking Gear: If you plan on hiking, include appropriate gear.

Language Phrasebook:

- Handy for basic communication.

Cultural Etiquette Research:

- Learn about local customs and manners.

Safety:

- Secure your belongings in hostels or crowded areas.

Emergency Whistle:

- For added safety during outdoor activities.

Remember, adapt this list based on your personal needs and the specific activities you plan to engage in during your backpacking trip through Lucca. Safe travels.

Currency and Banking

The official currency of Lucca is the euro (€). Euro coins and banknotes are accepted everywhere in the city, and can be used to pay for goods and services, including public transportation, admission to attractions, and dining out.

If you are traveling to Lucca from a country that does not use the euro, you will need to exchange your currency for euros before you arrive. You can do this at currency exchange bureaus or banks.

Currency Exchange Bureaus

Currency exchange bureaus are typically located in tourist areas, such as near airports, train stations, and major hotels. They offer competitive exchange rates and are usually convenient to use. However, it is important to compare rates at different bureaus before you exchange your money, as some may charge higher fees than others.

Banks

Banks also offer currency exchange services, but they may charge higher fees than currency exchange bureaus. Additionally, banks may have longer wait times and may require you to have a valid passport or other form of identification.

Here are some addresses of currency exchange bureaus and banks in Lucca:

Currency Exchange Bureaus:

- **Cambio Lucca:** Via Fillungo, 167, 55100 Lucca LU, Italy
- **Cambio Euro**: Piazza del Giglio, 2, 55100 Lucca LU, Italy
- **Cambio San Michele**: Via San Michele, 2, 55100 Lucca LU, Italy

Banks:

- **Banca Monte dei Paschi di Siena:** Piazza Santa Maria Corteorlandini, 5, 55100 Lucca LU, Italy
- **Banca Intesa Sanpaolo**: Piazza San Martino, 6, 55100 Lucca LU, Italy
- **Unicredit**: Via Fillungo, 272, 55100 Lucca LU, Italy

Banking Hours

Banks in Lucca are typically open from **8:30am** to **1:30pm**, **Monday through Friday**. However, some banks may have shorter hours on Saturdays or may be closed on Sundays.

ATMs

ATMs are widely available in Lucca and can be found in banks, hotels, and other tourist areas. ATMs accept most major credit and debit cards.

Credit and Debit Cards

Credit and debit cards are widely accepted in Lucca, but it is always a good idea to have some cash on hand, especially for smaller purchases.

Travelers Checks

Traveler's checks are not as widely accepted in Lucca as they once were, but they can still be exchanged for cash at some banks and currency exchange bureaus. However, it is important to note that you may have to pay a fee to exchange travelers checks.

Banking Services for Visitors

Visitors to Lucca can access a variety of banking services, including:

- **Cash Withdrawals:** Visitors can withdraw cash from ATMs using their credit or debit cards.
- **Currency Exchange:** Visitors can exchange foreign currency for euros at currency exchange bureaus or banks.
- **Traveler's Check Exchange:** Visitors can exchange traveler's checks for cash at some banks and currency exchange bureaus.
- **Money Transfers:** Visitors can send and receive money transfers through banks and money transfer services such as Western Union.
- **Check Cashing:** Some banks may cash personal checks for visitors, but they may charge a fee.

Tips for Managing Your Money in Lucca

Here are some tips for managing your money in Lucca:

1. Budget Carefully: Before you travel to Lucca, create a budget that includes your estimated expenses for food, accommodation, transportation, and activities.

2. Bring a Mix of Cash and Credit Cards: It is a good idea to bring a mix of cash and credit cards with you to Lucca. This will give you flexibility in case you encounter a situation where you cannot use your credit card.

3. Be Aware of Fees: Some banks and currency exchange bureaus may charge fees for services such as currency exchange and money transfers. Be sure to ask about fees before you make a transaction.

4. Keep your Valuables Safe: When you are not using your money or credit cards, keep them in a safe place such as your hotel safe or a money belt.

Following these tips will help you manage your money safely and effectively while you are visiting Lucca.

Safety Tips for Travelers

Lucca is a relatively safe city, but there are a few things visitors can do to stay safe and avoid any problems.

Here are some safety tips for visitors to Lucca:

1. Be Aware of your Surroundings: This is important in any city, but it's especially important in a tourist destination like Lucca. Pay attention to the people around you and be wary of anyone who seems to be following you or trying to distract you.

2. Keep your Valuables Close to you: Don't leave your purse or backpack unattended, and be careful with your wallet and phone. When you're walking around, keep your bag close to your body and don't put it in a basket or backpack that you carry on your back.

3. Don't Walk Alone at Night: It's best to avoid walking alone at night, especially in areas that you don't know well. If you do need to walk alone, try to stay on well-lit streets and be aware of your surroundings.

4. Be Careful with Pickpockets: Pickpockets are a problem in many tourist destinations, and Lucca is no exception. Be especially careful in crowded areas, such as markets and train stations.

5. Be Aware of Scams. There are a number of scams that target tourists in Lucca. One common scam is the "ring scam," where someone drops a ring at your feet and then pretends to help you find the owner. Another common scam is the "petition scam," where someone asks you to sign a petition and then tries to steal your money.

6. Be Careful when Crossing the Street: Lucca has a lot of narrow streets with cobblestones, and it can be easy to trip and fall. Be especially careful when crossing the street, and look both ways before crossing.

7. Be Aware of your Alcohol Consumption: Lucca is known for its wine, but it's important to drink responsibly. Don't drink too much alcohol, especially if you're going to be walking around at night.

8. Be Respectful of Local Customs: Lucca is a very traditional city, and it's important to be respectful of local customs. For example, dress modestly when visiting churches and other religious sites.

9. Learn a Few Basic Italian Phrases: This will help you communicate with locals and get around more easily.

If you do encounter a problem in Lucca, don't hesitate to contact the police or a trusted adult. The police in Lucca are generally very helpful, and they are there to protect tourists.

By following these safety tips, you can help ensure that you have a safe and enjoyable visit to Lucca.

Local Etiquette

When Visiting Lucca, understanding and respecting local etiquette becomes crucial for a more immersive and enriching experience, fostering positive interactions with the community and embracing the cultural nuances that make this Italian gem truly unique.. Here are a few tips:

1. Greetings:

- When greeting someone, it is customary to shake hands. If you are greeting a woman, it is polite to kiss her on the cheek.
- When addressing someone, use their formal title (e.g., Signor or Signora) and their last name.
- If you are meeting someone for the first time, it is polite to exchange business cards.

Dress Code:

- Lucca is a relatively conservative city, so it is important to dress modestly. Avoid wearing revealing clothing, especially when visiting religious sites.
- When visiting churches, it is required to cover your shoulders and knees.

Dining:

- When dining at a restaurant, it is customary to wait to be seated.
- Italians typically eat a light lunch and a larger dinner.
- It is considered polite to finish all of the food on your plate.
- If you are eating at a traditional Tuscan restaurant, be prepared to share your dishes with your fellow diners.
- When tipping, it is customary to leave 10-15% of the bill.

Other Tips:

- Be respectful of the local culture and customs.
- Avoid speaking loudly in public places.
- Do not litter.
- Be aware of your surroundings and take precautions to avoid pickpockets.

Here are some examples of how to use these etiquette tips in real-world situations:

- When greeting someone for the first time, you could say: **"Buongiorno, Piacere di conoscerla."** (Good morning, Nice to meet you.)
- If you are visiting a church, you should cover your shoulders and knees. You could bring a scarf or shawl to wrap around yourself, or you could wear a long skirt or dress.
- When dining at a restaurant, you should wait to be seated. You can usually do this by standing at the entrance of the restaurant and making eye contact with the host or hostess.

- If you are eating at a traditional Tuscan restaurant, you could share a dish with your fellow diners. This is a great way to try different foods and save money.
- When tipping, you can leave the tip in cash on the table or pay with your credit card and add the tip to the bill.
- Be on time. Punctuality is important in Italian culture, so it is considered rude to be late for appointments or social engagements.
- Be aware of your personal space. Italians typically stand closer to each other than people from other cultures, so be mindful of your personal space and avoid touching people unnecessarily.
- Don't be afraid to ask for help. If you are lost or need help with something, don't be afraid to ask a local for assistance. Italians are generally friendly and helpful people.

By following these tips, you can make a good impression on the locals and have a more enjoyable experience in Lucca.

Travel Insurance

For those on their first trip to Lucca, Italy, travel insurance is essential. But before you book your trip, it's important to make sure you have the right travel insurance.

Why do I need travel insurance for Lucca?

Travel insurance can protect you from a variety of unexpected events, such as:

1. Medical emergencies
2. Lost or stolen luggage
3. Canceled or delayed flights
4. Trip interruption
5. Natural disasters
6. Political unrest
7. Rental Car Coverage

It's especially important to have travel insurance when traveling to a foreign country, where medical costs can be high and you may not be familiar with the healthcare system.

What type of travel insurance do I need for Lucca?

There are many different types of travel insurance available, so it's important to choose a plan that meets your specific needs. Here are a few things to consider when choosing a travel insurance plan for Lucca:

- **Medical Coverage:** Make sure your plan covers medical emergencies, including hospitalization and repatriation.
- **Luggage Coverage**: Consider purchasing luggage coverage if you're checking bags on your flight, especially if you're packing valuable items.
- **Trip Cancellation and Interruption Coverage:** This coverage can reimburse you for the cost of your trip if it's canceled or interrupted due to an

unforeseen event, such as illness or flight cancellation.

- **Natural Disaster Coverage:** If you're traveling during hurricane season or to an area that is prone to earthquakes, consider purchasing natural disaster coverage.

How much does travel insurance to Lucca cost?

The cost of travel insurance to Lucca will vary depending on a number of factors, such as your age, the length of your trip, and the type of coverage you choose. However, you can expect to pay around **$10-$20** per day for a basic travel insurance plan.

How do I get travel insurance to Lucca?

There are a number of ways to purchase travel insurance. You can purchase it online, through a travel agent, or directly from an insurance company.

Here are a few tips for getting the best deal on travel insurance:

- **Compare quotes from multiple providers**: Don't just buy the first travel insurance plan you find. Take the time to compare quotes from multiple providers to make sure you're getting the best deal.

- **Consider purchasing a travel insurance policy that includes emergency medical evacuation**: This coverage can be very expensive if you need to be evacuated from Lucca for medical reasons.

- **Read the fine print carefully:** Before you purchase a travel insurance policy, be sure to read the fine print carefully to understand what is and isn't covered.

Here are some specific examples of how travel insurance can help you in Lucca:

- If you get sick or injured while traveling in Lucca, travel insurance can cover your medical bills.

- If your luggage is lost or stolen, travel insurance can reimburse you for the value of your belongings.

- If your flight is canceled or delayed, travel insurance can reimburse you for the cost of your flight and any additional expenses, such as hotel accommodations and meals.
- If you need to be evacuated from Lucca for medical reasons, travel insurance can cover the cost of your transportation.

How to get travel insurance prices

- There are a number of ways to get travel insurance prices. You can compare quotes online, through a travel agent, or directly from an insurance company.

- When getting travel insurance prices, be sure to compare quotes from multiple providers to make sure you're getting the best deal. Also, be sure to read the fine print carefully to understand what is and isn't covered.

In conclusion, travel insurance is an important part of any trip, especially if you're traveling to a foreign country. By purchasing travel insurance, you can protect yourself from unexpected events that could ruin your trip.

CHAPTER THREE

Getting to Lucca

By Flights

Lucca is served by Lucca-Tassignano Airport (PSA), also known as Galileo Galilei Airport. It is a small airport located about 5 kilometers (3.1 miles) from the city center.

The following major airlines operate flights to Lucca:

- British Airways
- EasyJet
- Ryanair
- Flights

There are direct flights to Lucca from a number of major European cities, including London, Manchester, and Paris. There are also connecting flights from many other cities around the world.

Here is a sample of flights to Lucca from major cities around the world:

This displays flight information for various cities, including departure and arrival times, as well as prices. London Heathrow offers a British Airways flight at 11:00 AM for **€109**, while London Gatwick provides an easyJet option departing at 10:00 AM for **€89**. Frankfurt's Lufthansa flight leaves at 12:00 PM, priced at **€129**. Dublin's Ryanair has a 10:30 AM departure for **€69**. Finally, New York's British Airways flight departs at 11:00 AM with a price of **€599**

Rules and Regulations

When flying to Lucca, it is important to be aware of the following rules and regulations:

- All passengers must have a valid passport and any other required travel documents.
- Passengers are allowed to check one bag and one carry-on item for free. Additional baggage may be subject to fees.

- Passengers must check in for their flight at least 2 hours before departure.
- Liquids, gels, and aerosols are limited to 100ml containers in carry-on luggage.
- Sharp objects and other potentially dangerous items are prohibited in carry-on luggage.

Getting from the Airport to Lucca

There are a number of ways to get from Lucca-Tassignano Airport to the city center:

1. Bus: There is a public bus that runs from the airport to the city center every 20 minutes. The bus ride takes about 20 minutes and costs **€2.50**.

2. Taxi: Taxis are available outside of the airport terminal. The taxi ride to the city center takes about 15 minutes and costs around **€20**.

3. Train: There is no train station at Lucca-Tassignano Airport. To take the train to Lucca, you will need to take a bus or taxi to the train station in Pisa. The train ride from Pisa to Lucca takes about 30 minutes and costs **€3.50**.

Travel Tips

Here are a few travel tips for flying to Lucca:

- Book your flight in advance, especially if you are traveling during peak season.
- Arrive at the airport at least 2 hours before your flight is scheduled to depart.
- Be aware of the baggage restrictions and make sure to pack light.
- Have your passport and other travel documents ready when you go through security.
- Purchase a Lucca Card before you arrive. This card will give you free admission to many of Lucca's top attractions, as well as unlimited use of public transportation.

I hope this guide has been helpful. Have a great trip to Lucca.

By Trains

List of regional trains serving Lucca, Italy

The most prevalent kind of train in Italy is a regional train, which connects all major cities and villages. Although they are often slower than high-speed trains, they are also more reasonably priced.

Regional trains that go to Lucca include:

Trains from major cities include

- Regionale Veloce (RV)
- Regionale (R).

The following trains go from significant Italian cities to Lucca:

- Regionale Veloce (RV) from Florence to Lucca
- Regionale Veloce (RV) from Pisa to Lucca
- Intercity (IC): From Rome to Lucca
- Intercity (IC) from Milan to Lucca
- Lucca to Naples: Intercity (IC)
- various trains

Trains that go to Lucca include:

- Train from Rome to Palermo at night, stopping in Lucca, is called the Trenitalia Pass Intercity Notte (ICN).

- Train that links the Cinque Terre communities to La Spezia, Pisa, and Lucca is called the Cinque Terre Express.

- The Cinque Terre Express is a train that runs between Lucca, La Spezia, and the Cinque Terre settlements.

In summary, Popular with tourists, Lucca has good rail connections to important Italian towns. Depending on your travel preferences and budget, there are several trains to select from.

Local Transportation

Italy's Tuscany region is home to the walled city of Lucca, which has a charming ancient district. It is a well-liked tourist site, and due to its tiny size, getting about is simple on foot. Buses, taxis, and rental bikes are only a few of the public transit alternatives offered, however.

Bus

In Lucca, the bus is the most widely used kind of public transit. Autolinee Toscane, the neighborhood bus operator, runs a network of routes that encircles the whole city.

You have two options for buying bus tickets: either you get on the bus and pay the driver up front, or you buy a ticket in advance from a newsstand or another approved outlet. Consider buying a pass if you anticipate using the bus regularly since it might end up saving you money over time.

The following is a list of Lucca's most well-traveled bus routes:

- **Lam Rossa**: This circuitous path around the inside of the city walls is a terrific way to take in the layout of the place.
- **Lam Verde**: This road runs from the city's heart to the bus and rail stations.
- **Lam Blu**: This road links Lucca's northern and eastern suburbs to the city center.
- **Lam Gialla**: This road links Lucca's central business district with its western and southern suburbs.

Taxi

Taxis are yet another practical means of transportation in Lucca. In the city, there are two primary taxi stands: one each in Piazza Santa Maria and Piazza Napoleone. You may also phone a taxi company to arrange a pickup or hail a cab on the street.

In Lucca, taxi costs are calculated using a meter, and the cost varies according to the route taken and the time of day..

Rental Bikes

You may hire a bike if you want a more active method to navigate about Lucca. Numerous bike rental outlets may be found all throughout the city.

Walking

The majority of the main attractions are situated within the city walls, making Lucca a fairly walkable city.

Segway Tours

A variety of businesses provide Segway tours in Lucca. This is a fantastic opportunity to see the city and discover its history.

Horse-Drawn Carriages

Many horse-drawn carriages are available for journeys around the city walls. Although it might be pricey, this is a lovely way to explore the city.

The cost breakdown for Lucca's numerous transportation alternatives is as follows:

- **€1.20 to €2.00** for each bus travel
- For a short trip within the city gates, a taxi costs **€10.00**.
- Rent a bike for **€10.00 to €20.00** per day.
- Tour on a Segway: around **€30.00** per person
- Horse-Drawn Carriage: A 30-minute trip costs around **€50**.

Conclusion, the ideal choice for you will rely on your unique demands and financial situation.

CHAPTER FOUR

Accommodation

Hotels and Resorts

Here are some of the best hotels and resorts in Lucca, along with their prices, locations, tips for getting there, and etiquette tips:

Best Western Grand Hotel Guinigi

This elegant hotel is located in the heart of Lucca, within walking distance of all the major attractions. It offers a variety of room types, including some with stunning views of the city walls and the Torre Guinigi, Lucca's famous tree-topped tower. Prices start at around €150 per night for a double room.

To get to the Best Western Grand Hotel Guinigi, take a taxi from the port to the Piazza dell'Anfiteatro. The hotel is located just off the piazza.

Etiquette Tips:

- The dress code at the Best Western Grand Hotel Guinigi is smart casual.

- Breakfast is included in the room rate.

- Check-in time is 2pm and check-out time is 12pm.

Albergo Celide

This upscale hotel is located in a quiet residential area of Lucca, just a short walk from the city center. It offers spacious and well-appointed rooms, a spa, a restaurant, and a bar. Prices start at around **€200** per night for a double room.

To get to the Albergo Celide, take a taxi from the port to the hotel's address (Viale Giuseppe Giusti, 25).

Etiquette tips:

- The dress code at the Albergo Celide is smart casual.

- Breakfast is included in the room rate.

- Check-in time is 2pm and check-out time is 12pm.

Hotel Villa La Principessa

This refined hotel is located in a beautiful park, just a short drive from Lucca. It offers elegant rooms and suites, an outdoor pool, and a chic restaurant. Prices start at around **€250** per night for a double room.

To get to Hotel Villa La Principessa, take a taxi from the port to the hotel's address (Via Nuova per Pisa, 1616G).

Etiquette tips:

- The dress code at Hotel Villa La Principessa is smart casual.
- Breakfast is included in the room rate.

- Check-in time is 2pm and check-out time is 12pm.

Resorts

Resort Dei Limoni

This family-friendly resort is located in the hills just outside of Lucca. It offers a variety of room types, including bungalows and apartments, as well as a swimming pool, a restaurant, and a bar. Prices start at around **€100** per night for a bungalow.

To get to Resort Dei Limoni, take a taxi from the port to the resort's address (Via della Chiesa, 102).

Etiquette tips:

- The dress code at Resort Dei Limoni is casual.

- Breakfast is included in the room rate.

- Check-in time is 2pm and check-out time is 12pm.

Agriturismo Fattoria Borgo la Torre

This charming agriturismo is located in the countryside just outside of Lucca. It offers rustic rooms and apartments, a swimming pool, a restaurant, and a bar. Prices start at around €120 per night for a double room.

To get to Agriturismo Fattoria Borgo la Torre, take a taxi from the port to the agriturismo's address (Via Borgo la Torre, 25).

Etiquette tips:

- The dress code at Agriturismo Fattoria Borgo la Torre is casual.
- Breakfast is included in the room rate.
- Check-in time is 2pm and check-out time is 12pm.
- Tips for getting to your hotel or resort from the port

The port of Lucca is located about 10 kilometers from the city center. The best way to get to your hotel or resort is by taxi. The taxi ride will take about **15** minutes and cost around **€20**.

Etiquette Tips for Staying in a Hotel or Resort in Lucca

- Italians are generally very friendly and welcoming, but it's always a good idea to be respectful of their culture and customs.
- When checking into your hotel or resort, be sure to greet the staff with a **"buongiorno"** (good morning) or **"buonasera"** (good evening).
- If you're staying in a hotel, be sure to leave a small tip for the housekeeping.

Charming Bed and Breakfasts

Lucca, Italy, is a beautiful walled city in Tuscany, and it's home to some of the most charming bed and breakfasts in the world. Here are they are:

Al Porto di Lucca B&B

- **Location**: Via Nottolini, 10, 55100 Lucca, Italy
- **Price**: Starting at €120 per night
- **Tips for getting there:** The B&B is located in the historic center of Lucca, just a short walk from the train station. If you're flying into Pisa International Airport, you can take a bus or train to Lucca. The B&B also offers a shuttle service from the airport for an additional fee.

- **Etiquette**: The B&B is a family-run business, and the owners are very welcoming and helpful. They're happy to provide recommendations for restaurants, attractions, and activities in Lucca.

Bed & Breakfast La Boheme

- **Location**: Via del Moro, 2, 55100 Lucca, Italy
- **Price**: Starting at €100 per night
- **Tips for getting there**: The B&B is located in the heart of Lucca's historic center, just a short walk from the Piazza dell'Anfiteatro and the

Piazza San Michele. If you're flying into Pisa International Airport, you can take a bus or train to Lucca. The B&B also offers a shuttle service from the airport for an additional fee.

- **Etiquette**: The B&B is a small, intimate establishment, and the owners take great pride in their guests' experience. They're happy to help you plan your itinerary and make reservations for restaurants and attractions.

L'Antica Bifore Guest House

- **Location**: Via Fillungo, 5, 55100 Lucca, Italy

- **Price**: Starting at €150 per night

- **Tips for getting there:** The B&B is located on Via Fillungo, Lucca's main shopping street. It's just a short walk from the train station and the Piazza dell'Anfiteatro. If you're flying into Pisa International Airport, you can take a bus or train to Lucca. The B&B also offers a shuttle service from the airport for an additional fee.

- **Etiquette**: The B&B is housed in a historic building, and the rooms are decorated with antique furniture and frescoes. The owners are very knowledgeable about the history of Lucca and Tuscany, and they're happy to share their insights with guests.

Villa La Bianca

- **Location**: Via della Zecca, 4, 55100 Lucca, Italy

- **Price**: Starting at **€200** per night

- **Tips for getting there:** Villa La Bianca is located just outside the historic center of Lucca, in a quiet residential neighborhood. It's a short walk from the train station and the Piazza dell'Anfiteatro. If you're flying into Pisa International Airport, you can take a bus or train to Lucca. The B&B also offers a shuttle service from the airport for an additional fee.

- **Etiquette**: Villa La Bianca is a luxury bed and breakfast, and the owners offer their guests a high level of service. They're happy to help you plan your itinerary, make reservations for restaurants and attractions, and arrange transportation.

Ride to the Charming Bed and Breakfasts

Once you arrive in Lucca, you have a few options for getting to your bed and breakfast. If you're staying in the historic center, you can walk to most of the bed and breakfasts. If you're staying outside the historic center, you can take a taxi or bus.

Here are some tips for getting to your bed and breakfast by taxi:

- Make sure to agree on a price with the taxi driver before you get in the car.
- The taxi driver should drop you off at the door of your bed and breakfast.
- It's customary to tip the taxi driver 10-15%.

Here are some tips for getting to your bed and breakfast by bus:

- You can buy tickets at the bus station or on the bus.
- Be sure to check the bus schedule before you go, so you know when the bus will arrive.
- The bus will drop you off at the nearest bus stop to your bed and breakfast.
- Once you arrive at your bed and breakfast, be sure to check in with the owner or manager. They will give you your room key and show you around.

Etiquette

Here are some tips for etiquette at a charming bed and breakfast:

- Be respectful of the other guests and the owner's property.
- Keep noise to a minimum, especially early in the morning and late at night.

84

- Be tidy in the common areas, such as the dining room and
- Clean up after yourself in the kitchen.
- Be on time for breakfast.
- Let the owner know if you need anything or have any special requests.
- Leave a tip for the staff (if there is any).
- Avoid wearing strong perfumes or colognes.
- Be mindful of your food allergies or dietary restrictions.

In conclusion, if you're looking for a charming bed and breakfast to stay in, you're sure to find something to your taste. Be sure to follow the etiquette tips above to make sure you have a pleasant and enjoyable stay.

Budget-Friendly Options

Accommodation:

- Dorm beds at the Hostel Pisa Tower start at €20 per night.

- According to Airbnb, shared homes or rooms cost between **€30** and **€60** per night.

Food:

- Popular neighborhood restaurant Trattoria da Leo offers pasta meals for between **$8** and **$12**.
- Pizzas at Il Mecenate start at only **€7**.

Transportation:

- **Cycling**: Renting a bike for a day costs around **€10** to **€15**, and it's a terrific way to see the city.

Attractions:

- Free to use for biking or walking, the Lucca Walls provide stunning city views.
- San Michele in Foro Church: Around **€3** for admission.

Entertainment:

- **Piazza dell'Anfiteatro:** Free entertainment in a buzzing setting.

- **Ideally, Lucca Comics & Games will:** A few events are free, while ticket costs range.

Shopping:

- **Local Markets:** For inexpensive gifts and fresh fruit, check out Mercato del Carmine or Mercato di Sant'Ambrogio.

Miscellaneous:

- Gelateria Veneta: Treat yourself to delectable gelato for around **$2–$4.**

A pleasant experience is available in Lucca without spending a fortune!

CHAPTER FIVE

Culinary Delights

Local Cuisine and Specialties

The Italian city of Lucca, located in the heart of Tuscany, has a thriving culinary sector that honors the area's extensive culinary history. The native food in Lucca is a delicious fusion of classic Italian tastes that uses only the best, freshest ingredients. Here is a list of some regional specialities that make up Lucca's culinary scene:

1. Buccellato: A ring-shaped bread stuffed with raisins and anise seeds, is the sweet specialty of Lucca. This delicious treat is a representation of the region's baking prowess and is often consumed during festive events.

2. Farro Soup: In Luccan cuisine, the ancient grain farro is the star ingredient. Farro soup, sometimes referred to as "zuppa di farro," is a substantial meal made with this wholesome grain and frequently includes vegetables, legumes, and flavorful herbs.

3. Tordelli Lucchesi: This is a ravioli-like sort of filled pasta. Typically, meat, cheese, and spinach are combined to fill Tordelli Lucchesi, making them a delicious treat. A thick ragù sauce is often served with them.

4. Olive Oil: Lucca is famous for its premium olive oil, which is common across Tuscany. In Lucan kitchens, the native olive oil, with its rich taste and golden color, is a mainstay and is drizzled over salads, pasta, and grilled meats.

5. Cecina: A thin, crispy pancake made from chickpea flour, cecina is a well-known street snack in Lucca. Both residents and tourists may enjoy this salty and filling snack, which is seasoned with rosemary and salt.

6. Castagnaccio: A traditional treat in Lucca is this cake made with chestnut flour. It often has pine nuts, rosemary, and raisins added to give it a distinctive and earthy taste.

7. Wines from Lucca: The area around Lucca is well-known for its wines. Sangiovese, Trebbiano, and Vermentino are a few of the distinguished kinds. With their own regional qualities, these wines enhance the dining experience by harmoniously blending with the area food.

Overall, investigating Lucca's culinary offers is a voyage into the heart of Tuscan traditions, where each dish narrates the history and agricultural bounty of the area.

Top-Rated Restaurants and Cafés

The food scene of Lucca, which is known for its picturesque medieval walls and cobblestone lanes, is a delicious fusion of classic Tuscan tastes with contemporary innovation. Here are a few of the top-rated eateries that stand out in this culinary paradise:

1. Buca di Sant'Antonio: It is a renowned restaurant recognized for its wonderful Tuscan fare. It is located right in the center of Lucca. This restaurant embodies the spirit of regional cuisine with dishes like decadent pasta with truffle infusion and flavorful bistecca alla fiorentina.

2. Giglio Rosso: If you're looking for a more modern dining experience, Giglio Rosso wows with its creative taste fusions and presentation. The cuisine offers a gastronomic experience that surprises and delights, with inventive takes on classic foods.

3. Osteria Miranda: It is renowned for its excellent seafood and pleasant atmosphere. It is nestled away in a charming area of Lucca. A special dining experience is ensured by Osteria Miranda's dedication to using only the freshest, highest-quality ingredients.

4. Gli Orti di Via Elisa: Gli Orti di Via Elisa is a paradise for vegetarians and vegans. This eatery creates colorful, plant-based cuisine that honor the bounty of regional agriculture while satisfying a wide variety of dietary requirements.

5. La Mora: A family-run business, La Mora exudes friendliness and sincerity. It is a location where ancient recipes, handed down through generations, come to life on the plate and specializes in rustic Tuscan cuisine.

6. Caffè Di Simo: Lucca's café tradition is alive and well at Caffè Di Simo, where beautifully made coffee is combined with mouth watering pastries. This beautiful café welcomes you to appreciate the straightforward pleasures of Italian coffee culture, whether you're looking for a leisurely breakfast or a quick espresso pick-me-up.

Each mouthful of food that is consumed while exploring Lucca's culinary landscape is a cultural experience that combines tradition with innovation and a passion for delicious cuisine.

Farmers' Markets and Food Festivals

Lucca is a beautiful city in Tuscany, Italy, and is well known for its thriving farmers' markets and food festivals that honor the area's rich culinary tradition. These gatherings include the finest regional foods, including handcrafted treats and time-honored traditions.

1. Market at Piazza dell'Anfiteatro: The Piazza dell'Anfiteatro, which is located within Lucca's ancient walls, is home to a weekly farmers' market that turns the area into a lively center for culinary treats. Local farmers display their seasonal fruits, veggies, and flavorful herbs with pride, producing a rainbow of hues and tastes.

2. Lucca Antique Market with Food Stalls: This distinctive market mixes the draw of regional food with the charm of antiques. While enjoying mouthwatering street cuisine, stroll through cobblestone lanes dotted with antiques. The marriage of historical inventiveness and culinary creativity produces a remarkable experience, from porchetta sandwiches to freshly baked pastries.

3. Olive Oil Festival In Lucca: It pays homage to the area's olive fields while celebrating Tuscany's "liquid gold." Extra virgin olive oils are available for sampling, and each one reflects the unique qualities of the regional olive varieties. Along with tastings coupled with local wines, the event also provides lessons on the manufacture of olive oil.

4. Lucca Summer Event: It is largely a music event, but it also has a culinary component. Performances by famous performers are accompanied by food booths serving local dishes from Tuscany like ribollita and al pomodoro, resulting in a delicious fusion of music and cuisine.

5. Lucca Wine and Grape Festival: This honors the great wines of the area against the background of Lucca's historic buildings. Local trattorias provide food to go along with the wide range of wines, while vineyards from the neighboring hills present their best vintages. Live music, conventional dancing, and customs including grape-stomping are all part of the celebrations.

6. Lucca Chocolate Festival: Those with a sweet craving will find the Lucca Chocolate Festival to be a paradise of delight. Chocolatiers from all around Italy come together to showcase their best works, from luxurious truffles to handcrafted bars. Visitors are enticed to discover the world of great chocolate by the streets' alluring cocoa fragrance.

Farmers' markets and food festivals in Lucca are more than just gatherings; they are celebrations of the area's agrarian abundance and culinary ability. These gatherings play a crucial role in the cultural fabric of Lucca since residents and tourists mix there while delicious fragrances permeate the city's historic streets.

Street Food

Lucca, a city renowned for its ancient walls and attractive alleyways, provides a mouthwatering selection of street cuisine that tempts both residents and tourists' taste buds. The dynamic street food scene reflects the rich culinary tradition of Tuscany with savory snacks and sweet sweets.

1. Panino al Lampredotto (€5–€7): Tuck into a crusty roll stuffed with delicious (cow gut), a local delicacy. It's a delicious treat when served with a splash of salsa verde.

2. Cecina (3–4 euro): Cecina is a thin, delicious pancake made from chickpea flour. It's a cheap and well-liked street food that is sometimes seasoned with rosemary.

3. Torta di Riso ($2-$3): This rice pudding tart is a fantastic alternative for people with a sweet craving. It is a delicacy you must taste because of its creamy texture and subdued sweetness.

4. Arancini (€1.5–€2): These golden rice balls loaded with ragù, peas, and cheese bring Sicilian flavor to Lucca's streets. both inexpensive and rewarding.

5. Schiacciata con l'uva (€3–€4): Enjoy this delicious flatbread with grapes on top. It showcases the fresh fruit from the area and finds the ideal mix between sweet and savory.

6. Bomboloni (€1–€2): Indulge in these delicious Italian doughnuts that are stuffed to the brim with custard, chocolate, or fruit jam. A delicious treat that is reasonably priced.

7. Spiedino di carne (€4–€6): A heartier choice is grilled beef skewers. These skewers are an excellent pick for grab-and-go meals, whether they include tasty beef or luscious pig.

8. gelato (€2.5–€4): No street food experience is complete without the gelaterias in Lucca that provide a wide selection of varieties so you can enjoy the true flavor of Italian ice cream.

In conclusion, let your taste sensations lead you on this gastronomic trip, where each mouthful narrates a tale of tradition and flavor, as you meander around Lucca's picturesque alleyways.

CHAPTER SIX

Shopping in Lucca

Artisan Shops

Lucca, a charming town in Tuscany, boasts a vibrant array of artisan shops, each contributing to the city's rich cultural tapestry.

1. Bottega del Fabbro: This blacksmith's haven showcases intricate ironwork, from hand-forged gates to delicate sculptures.

2. La Corte Miracoli: A gem for pottery enthusiasts, offering a kaleidoscope of hand-painted ceramics reflecting the region's traditional motifs.

3. L'Angolo del Tessitore: Step into this weaving paradise, where skilled artisans craft luxurious textiles, from vibrant tapestries to delicate linens.

4. Arte del Vetro: A mesmerizing display of Murano glass awaits at this studio, where artisans shape molten glass into exquisite chandeliers, vases, and jewelry.

5. Il Taglialegna: Woodwork aficionados find solace here, surrounded by finely carved furniture, ornate sculptures, and bespoke wooden instruments.

6. Penna La Carta e: A haven for stationery connoisseurs, offering artisanal paper and handcrafted quills, reminiscent of an era when writing was an art form.

7. Del Ceramista La Fornace: Dive into the world of ceramics, where skilled potters mold clay into functional masterpieces, from rustic tableware to intricately designed tiles.

8. Oreficeria d'Arte: Adorn yourself with elegance from this jewelry boutique, where local goldsmiths fashion exquisite pieces inspired by Lucca's history and landscapes.

9. Antichi Sapori: Beyond tangible art, savor the artistry of flavors with this artisanal food shop, offering Tuscan delicacies, olive oils, and aged balsamic vinegars.

10. Stamperia del Lione: Witness the revival of traditional printing techniques at this charming print shop, producing handcrafted paper and unique prints.

These artisan shops not only showcase the mastery of their craftsmen but also invite visitors to take home a piece of Lucca's artistic soul.

High-End Boutiques

Lucca, a lovely city in Tuscany, Italy, has a number of upscale stores that give its ancient streets a touch of elegance. With a blend of modern design and classic Italian workmanship, each store provides a distinctive shopping experience.

1. Boutique del Cashmere: Known for its magnificent cashmere clothing, this store features the best Italian workmanship in the production of sumptuous sweaters, scarves, and shawls. Elegant people are drawn to the gentle textures and classic patterns.

3. Dolce Vita Shoes: For those who appreciate fine Italian leather work, Dolce Vita Shoes is a refuge. This shop makes sure that every step is made with the highest elegance and comfort, from chic boots to custom loafers.

4. Galleria degli Abiti: It is a high-end apparel store that carries a carefully chosen selection of designer clothes from well-known Italian and foreign fashion firms. It is a destination for those looking for expensive, cutting-edge clothing.

5. Oro e Argento's Best: Invest in some of Oro e Argento's best jewelry to adorn yourself. This store specializes in exquisite, one-of-a-kind accessories made from handmade gold and silver with precious stones.

6. La Profumeria Elegante: La Profumeria Elegante is a store that specializes in high-end scents. Indulge your senses here. This store provides an olfactory experience for people with a discriminating nose, including everything from vintage aromas to niche perfumes.

7. Enoteca dei Tessuti: Offering an opulent array of textiles and materials, this store combines fashion with home décor. This shop serves people wishing to add a touch of luxury to their living spaces with lavish curtains and custom linens.

8. La Camiceria Finissima: This store elevates men's style and is known for its custom shirts and suits. La Camiceria Finissima is a refuge for males looking for individualized flair and sartorial brilliance.

9. Bella Vita Art Gallery: This gallery mixes art and luxury in addition to fashion. This boutique enables customers to take home a piece of creative refinement, whether it be a painting, sculpture, or limited-edition print, by showcasing the works of regional and worldwide artists.

10. Cucina Chic: For foodies, Cucina Chic provides a hand-picked assortment of upscale cookware and fine ingredients. This shop caters to individuals who value the finest things in cuisine, from artisan cookware to rare truffles.

11. Vino Prestigio: Wine lovers may delve into the world of premium wines there. This boutique gives wine aficionados the chance to savor the robust tastes and scents of Italy's most prominent vineyards by offering a large selection of rare and older wines.

In summary, Visitors may immerse themselves in the pinnacle of luxury and cultural riches thanks to Lucca's upscale stores, which together weave a tapestry of sophisticated tastes in everything from fashion and art to literature and food.

Souvenirs and Unique Finds

Tuscany's lovely town of Lucca is teeming with trinkets and one-of-a-kind items that perfectly encapsulate the region's rich history and culture.

1. Olive Oil: Lucca is famous for its premium olive oil, which is common across Tuscany. Look for extra virgin olive oil that is produced locally; it is sometimes sold in beautifully designed bottles.

2. Items with a Puccini Theme: As the birthplace of renowned composer Giacomo Puccini, Lucca provides a selection of trinkets that are motivated by his legacy. Music lovers will discover lovely gifts, from sheet music to odd Puccini-themed goods.

3. Mementos from the Lucca Comics & Games Event: If you come during the Lucca Comics & Games event, be sure to get some special mementos. The treasures from this highly regarded event are one-of-a-kind mementos since it honors gaming, animation, and comics.

4. Handmade Pasta and Culinary Delights: Look for handmade pasta, goods with truffle flavoring, and Tuscan spices at your neighborhood stores. These delectable treasures showcase the area's superior cuisine.

5. Antique Maps and Prints: Lucca has a long history, and old maps and prints that show how the town has changed make interesting wall décor or valuable collectibles.

6. Buccellato: A speciality of Lucca, this classic sweet bread. You may be guaranteed to have a taste of the town's culinary tradition by bringing home a fresh Buccellato.

7. Lucca Marble: Take a look at and buy little sculptures or decorations made of the prized Carrara marble, demonstrating the creative workmanship of the area.

8. Products Made of Linen: Tuscany is renowned for its fine linen. Look for mementos that capture the grandeur of Tuscany in handcrafted linens, such as tablecloths, shirts, and napkins.

9. Wine & Wine Accessories: Look for Tuscan wines at nearby wineries or specialist stores. For a stylish memento of your trip to Lucca, pair it with distinctive wine accessories like handmade corkscrews or wine glasses.

10. Items with a Bicycle Theme: Cycling is a great way to see Lucca's well-preserved Renaissance walls. To remember the city's bicycle-friendly culture, think about purchasing souvenirs with a cycling motif, such as prints and accessories.

So whether you're drinking Tuscan wine or admiring old maps, the mementos of Lucca are more than simply something to have; they're gateways to Tuscany, letting you take a piece of this fascinating town wherever you go.

CHAPTER SEVEN

Events and Festivals

Lucca Summer Festival

The picturesque Italian town of Lucca is transformed into a platform for some of the greatest names in music by the Lucca Summer Festival, a musical spectacle. This yearly occasion, usually celebrated in July, has come to be associated with balmy summer evenings packed with exhilarating entertainment.

The festival's distinctive attractiveness comes from its blending of modern music with aesthetic history. The ancient walls and cobblestone alleys of Lucca provide for a beautiful background for the wide variety of performers that perform there. The roster, which includes well-known rock bands and pop wonders, appeals to a wide range of musical preferences, drawing music lovers from all over the world.

Despite having famous performers as guests, Lucca Summer Festival stands out for its cozy environment. The concertgoers may enjoy top-notch music while surrounded by centuries-old architecture thanks to the stages' thoughtful placement inside the historic town center. The fusion of contemporary sounds with antiquated settings produces a mystical atmosphere that reverberates long after the last note has faded.

With the help of great performers like Elton John, The Rolling Stones, and Bob Dylan over the years, Lucca Summer Festival has grown to become a must-attend occasion for both music lovers and artists. The festival not only puts music front and center, but it also celebrates cross-cultural interchange by bringing people from all over the globe together to enjoy the common language of music.

Insummary, the Lucca Summer Festival, an incredible celebration of music that leaves an imprint on everyone who has the luxury of being a part of this musical adventure, is essentially a harmonic fusion of timeless beauty and modern rhythm.

Luminara di Santa Croce

Lucca's Luminara di Santa Croce is a mesmerizing display that illuminates the city with a warm, golden light. On the evening of September 13, Lucca is transformed into a captivating sea of flickering candles as a result of this yearly celebration. The festival has a strong religious significance and is steeped in history.

The Church of Santa Croce, a masterpiece of architecture and the center of the Luminara, is located in the center of the festival. Thousands of candles are painstakingly placed along the complex cathedral exterior as twilight falls, producing beautiful patterns of light and shadow. The end effect is nothing short of breathtaking, as the historical surroundings take on a surreal appearance thanks to the candles' soothing radiance.

The celebration honors the Feast of the Exaltation of the Holy Cross, and the candlelight setting represents the spiritual and religious light. Both residents and pilgrims congregate to see this otherworldly change, sharing an experience that cuts across generations. The Luminara di Santa Croce is more than just a beautiful sight; it is a symbol of Lucca's deep ties to history and cultural diversity.

Walking through the Luminara's lit streets, it's impossible not to be enchanted by the magical ambiance. A special spell is cast on the city by the interaction of light and shadow, transforming an ordinary evening into a profound trip through religion and history. Lucca exhibits its ageless beauty and the resilient character of a society that values its history in the warm light of the illuminated streets.

Comics and Games Convention

Every year in the quaint Italian city of Lucca, a colorful pop culture event called the Lucca Comics & Games Convention takes place. The conference, one of the biggest of its type in Europe, expertly combines the gaming, entertainment, and comic book industries to provide fans and newbies alike an immersive experience.

With its ancient walls and charming history, Lucca offers a distinctive setting for this meeting of imaginative people and ardent supporters. The event features a wide variety of comic books, graphic novels, and manga, attracting creators from all over the world. The chance to interact with beloved artists, take part in panel discussions, and discover the newest releases is available to attendees. But Lucca Comics & Games extends beyond printed media. It welcomes the vibrant and always changing gaming industry. The conference offers a wide variety of games, from classic board games to cutting-edge electronic games.

The event's interactive exhibitions, competitions, and sneak peeks of forthcoming releases give it an exciting new dimension and help to build a feeling of community among gamers. Cosplayers play a big part in converting Lucca into a vibrant mosaic of characters from popular comic books, video games, and movies. The streets come alive with painstakingly made costumes, providing spectators with a visual feast and fostering an inclusive environment where everyone can share their love of fandom.

Beyond the convention center's bustle, the city itself turns into a center of activity. In order to accommodate the rush of tourists, Lucca organizes events, movies, and themed exhibits all throughout its ancient alleyways. The convention has an effect on the city and the many people who find inspiration and connection in its energetic and innovative areas long after the event dates have passed.

CHAPTER EIGHT

Rich History and Culture

Lucca's Music Tradition

The music of Lucca permeates the charming city's cobblestone streets and old buildings, capturing the spirit of Italian cultural diversity. Lucca, renowned for its rich musical history, has created a legacy that reaches well beyond its medieval fortifications.

The renowned composer Giacomo Puccini, a local son whose operatic works, like "La Bohème" and "Madama Butterfly," continue to enthrall audiences worldwide, is at the center of Lucca's musical identity. The annual Puccini Festival honors this musical giant and draws fans from all over the world to the large open-air theater next to Lake Massaciuccoli.

Beyond Puccini, Lucca's historic cathedrals provide a beautiful setting for classical performances, demonstrating the city's dedication to maintaining its musical legacy. The Lucca Classical Music Festival, presented in these historic locations, weaves together the works of both ancient and new composers like a sonorous tapestry. During the Lucca Summer Festival, a vibrant showcase showcasing worldwide musicians from many genres, the streets of Lucca come alive with the sounds of folk music. The city resounds with a symphony of various musical expressions, from the timeless melodies of the Lucca Philharmonic Orchestra to the vivid notes of local street artists.

Although largely a pop culture festival, the renowned Lucca Comics & Games Festival incorporates the musical realm with live performances and themed concerts, illuminating the meeting point of music and fantasy within the city's cultural tapestry.

Overall, the rich musical legacy of Lucca permeates more than just formal performances; it also permeates the city's thriving café scene, where mellow guitar chords and singing add to the day-to-day ambience. Every note that resonates through Lucca's historic streets proudly tells its musical tale, asking everyone who comes to hear it to join in on the city's timeless tune.

Architectural Marvels and Landmarks

Lucca, which is located in Tuscany, has a diverse collection of architectural wonders and historical sites. The massive Lucca Cathedral, a magnificent illustration of Italian Gothic architecture, is unquestionably the gem in the city's crown. The complex front of this building, which is embellished with sculptures and reliefs, is a testament to both its creative prowess and religious importance. A remarkable and lush sight against the skyline is the Torre Guinigi, a medieval tower next to the cathedral that is topped with holm oaks.

Visitors are rewarded with panoramic views of the city after ascending its historic stairs, which reveal a maze of terracotta rooftops and secret piazzas. Amazingly well-preserved defense walls surround Lucca like a well-worn hug. A leisurely bike ride or walk over these ramparts provides a window into the city's strategic history and the opportunity to be in awe of the magnificent surroundings beyond. With its lively vitality, the Piazza dell'Anfiteatro, an oval plaza that mimics the design of the old Roman amphitheaters, captivates. The fact that it is surrounded by quaint cafés and historic structures is evidence of Lucca's skill in fusing the past with the present.

The Basilica of San Frediano, with its mosaic-covered front and beautiful golden mosaic representing the Ascension of Christ, draws to lovers of Romanesque architecture. Explore the space to find a treasure of religious art and an ethereal atmosphere. The allure of Lucca goes beyond its civic and ecclesiastical institutions. An example of the city's aristocratic heritage is the lavish palace and beautiful gardens known as the

Palazzo Pfanner. Every antique structure and cobblestone street in Lucca tells a tale about a period of Italian history, making it a paradise for individuals who are fascinated by the meeting point of time and architecture.

Museums and Galleries

Lucca, which is located in the center of Tuscany, has a rich cultural tapestry made of historical and artistic influences. The museums and galleries of the city act as stewards of its illustrious past and invite tourists to explore the tales etched into their surfaces.

The National Museum in the Palazzo Mansi is a treasure trove of artwork and relics that provides a window into the sumptuous way of life of Lucca's aristocratic families. The amazing collection of paintings, sculptures, and decorative arts that are shown there spans centuries, and its corridors reverberate with the voices of the past.

The Puccini Museum honors legendary composer Giacomo Puccini, a Lucca native, for those mesmerized by the symphony of strings. This little museum, housed in Puccini's old home, takes visitors into the life of the maestro by showcasing mementos, musical scores, and personal items. As one enters the Lucca Center for Contemporary Art (Lu.C.C.A.), one may see how modernism is framed by the historic city walls. This vibrant venue exhibits contemporary artwork and offers a forum for regional and international artists to engage in a conversation about innovation and tradition.

The Cathedral Museum is another example of Lucca's dedication to upholding its cultural character. Here, ecclesiastical art has a prominent position. Visitors may see sculptures, paintings, and holy artifacts that each depict a stage of Lucca's spiritual development. The National Villa Guinigi Museum is a breath of fresh air. This museum, which houses sculptures and antiques in a peaceful environment, is tucked away in a garden surrounded by old oak trees and a tower with holm oaks growing on top.

In Lucca's gallery-lit streets, the past and present coexist together, enticing visitors to discover the historical strokes that have painted this beautiful city.

CHAPTER NINE

Outdoor Adventures

Biking and Hiking Trails

Lucca, a charming Italian city renowned for its well-preserved Renaissance walls, offers a splendid array of biking and hiking trails that weave through picturesque landscapes and historic sites.

1. Lucca City Walls: Start your journey with a ride or walk along the city walls. The wide promenade atop the fortifications provides breathtaking views of the city and its surroundings.

2. Serchio River Park Trail: Follow the Serchio River as it winds through lush greenery. This trail is ideal for both biking and hiking, offering a peaceful escape from the urban hustle.

3. Monti Pisani Trails: Head south to explore the trails around the Monti Pisani, a mountain range near Lucca. These trails vary in difficulty, catering to both casual strollers and avid hikers.

4. Matraia Loop: Venture into the hills and embark on the Matraia Loop. This trail combines the beauty of nature with historical charm, passing through quaint villages and olive groves.

5. Garfagnana Valley Path: For a more challenging hike or bike ride, the Garfagnana Valley Path presents rugged terrain with rewarding panoramic views of the Apuan Alps.

6. Valli di Lucca Loop: Experience the diverse landscapes surrounding Lucca with the Valli di Lucca Loop. From vineyards to chestnut forests, this trail showcases the region's agricultural richness.

7. San Rossore Nature Reserve: Explore the coastal side of Lucca with trails in the San Rossore Nature Reserve. Pine forests and sand dunes characterize this area, providing a unique setting for outdoor enthusiasts.

8. Montecarlo Wine Trail: Combine your love for biking with wine tasting along the Montecarlo Wine Trail. This leisurely route introduces you to the region's vineyards and wine-making heritage.

Whether you're a cycling enthusiast or a nature lover seeking hiking adventures, Lucca's diverse trails promise a delightful journey through Tuscany's natural and cultural wonders.

Day Trips to Surrounding Areas

Lucca provides a wide range of fascinating day excursions to the region's surroundings that highlight Tuscany's diverse natural and cultural landscape.

1. Pisa: The famous Leaning Tower of Pisa, a UNESCO World Heritage site, is just a short drive away. Admire the architectural marvels as you go around the church and Piazza dei Miracoli.

2. Experience Florence's Renaissance Beauty: it's just a short train ride away. Visit the Ponte Vecchio, the Uffizi Gallery, and the magnificent Florence Cathedral.

3. Cinque Terre: Cinque Terre is a little farther away but is well worth the drive since it provides vibrant cliffside towns, hiking paths, and spectacular vistas of the Ligurian Sea.

4. Garfagnana Area: Nature enthusiasts will enjoy a day trip to the Garfagnana area. Discover the Apuan Alps, stop by quaint towns like Barga, and savor regional food.

5. Versilia Coast: Visit the Versilia Coast for a day at the beach. Sand beaches and a bustling promenade are available in Viareggio, a city famous for its carnival.

6. Chianti Wine Area: Tour the Chianti wine area to experience the tastes of Tuscany. Experience top-notch wine and beautiful vineyard scenery.

7. Montecatini Terme: Relax at the thermal resort town of Montecatini Terme, which is renowned for its therapeutic waters and opulent architecture.

8. Lucca's Villa: Explore the villas in the area, such as Villa Reale and Villa Grabau, which have beautiful gardens and noteworthy pasts.

9. Siena: Another jewel of Tuscany is Siena, which has the Piazza del Campo, the magnificent Siena Cathedral, and a medieval cityscape.

10. Bagni di Lucca: Discover the allure of Bagni di Lucca, a town renowned for its hot spas and the charming Ponte delle Catene bridge.

Every tourist will discover something special on these day excursions from Lucca, which offer a wide variety of experiences from cultural immersion to natural beauty.

Adventure Sports

An exciting selection of adventure sports are available in Lucca, an attractive city in Tuscany, Italy, to suit a variety of interests. The Lucca Walls, a distinctive aspect of the city, provide cyclists a beautiful route to go. The well-maintained Renaissance walls provide a fantastic bicycle path with sweeping views of the city and its surroundings. The adjacent Apuan Alps provide paragliding, a must-try activity for those seeking an adrenaline thrill. The breathtaking scenery combined with the thrill of flying through the air provide priceless memories. Spelunking in the area's caves, including the Grotta del Vento, where stalactites and stalagmites reveal a fascinating subterranean world, is another option for the adventurous.

The Serchio River's proximity to Lucca makes water-based experiences possible. The rapids of the river may be navigated by kayakers and rafters who want to take in the natural splendor of the Tuscan landscape. The Serchio also extends an invitation to the brave to try their hand at canyoning, a water activity that combines rock climbing, swimming, and abseiling.

The Apuan Alps provide tough tracks through verdant woods and meadows that give mountain riding a whole new meaning. Another adjacent mountain range called the Apennines offers excellent climbing and trekking terrain, as well as stunning views and opportunities to interact with the region's varied flora and animals. The adventure sports culture in Lucca is widespread and serves as a center for outdoor lovers. Lucca entices thrill-seekers to enjoy the adrenaline of its diverse landscapes, whether riding atop historic walls, flying through the air, or negotiating river rapids.

Relaxing by the River

The picturesque town of Lucca is located in the heart of Tuscany, and the River Serchio delicately flows its way through it, providing a calm retreat for visitors seeking peace. Relaxing by Lucca's riverbanks is an extraordinary sensory experience that will immerse you in a kaleidoscope of sights, sounds, and feelings.

The river's steady flow transforms into a soothing lullaby as the golden sun sets beyond the horizon, bathing the surface in a warm light. Framed by historic bridges with moss-covered stones, the area has an air of timeless grandeur about it. The air is permeated with the delicate scent of flowering flowers, adding to the symphony of the senses. An easy walk down the river's bank offers charming eateries and secret nooks where one may take a moment to take in the lovely surroundings. A soundtrack reflecting the lively character of Lucca is created by the beautiful blending of the murmur of conversations and the odd burst of laughter.

A feeling of history is evoked by the town's ancient walls, which surround it and stand as mute witnesses to centuries of history. The riverbanks provide a natural haven—a getaway from the hectic pace of contemporary life—decorated with weeping willows and cypress trees. The water reflects the sky's shifting colors as you relax into a peaceful moment, producing a spellbinding reflection that captures the heart. Ducks gently move over the water's surface, giving the image a lovely rhythm. The passage of time appears to stop, allowing for reflection and a profound appreciation of the basic pleasures offered by nature.

Unwinding by the River of Lucca goes beyond simple leisure; it transforms into a lyrical contact with nature, a call to relax and appreciate the beautiful beauty embedded into the very fabric of this alluring Italian town.

CHAPTER TEN

Top Attractions

Lucca's City Walls

The majestic City Walls of Lucca serve as a reminder of the city's significant strategic role throughout history. These Renaissance-era defenses, which were constructed during the 16th and 17th centuries, perfectly capture Lucca's enduring allure and tenacity.

The four-kilometer-long walls were first built to protect the city from outside dangers, a reflection of the turbulent times of political unrest in Italy. Because they developed into a multipurpose area, Lucca's defenses were more than only practical. A tree-lined promenade has been built on the wide tops of the walls today, resulting in a distinctive fusion of ancient architecture with recreational space.

Panorama views of Lucca's charming cityscape, with its red-tiled roofs and harmoniously rising medieval towers, may be seen when strolling around the city walls. The Guinigi Tower, which is surrounded by oak trees, stands out as a reminder of a time when aristocratic families strove to flaunt their money and status via elaborate architecture.

The walls still hold strong after centuries of change, including political upheavals and cultural revolutions, and they provide a concrete link to Lucca's history. The walls and bastions, which were once essential for defense, are today used as venues for festivals, concerts, and other cultural events that liven up the city. Beyond its importance in terms of history and culture, Lucca's City Walls represent the peaceful cohabitation of the old and the modern. Both locals and visitors find comfort in roaming atop these ancient defenses, which makes them more than simply a sign of safety but also a tangible illustration of Lucca's capacity for adaptation and historical adulation.

Historical Significance

The Italian city of Lucca, which is tucked away in Tuscany, has a rich history that spans many centuries. Although its roots may be found in Etruscan times, the medieval age is when it really blossomed. With its still-standing Renaissance walls, Lucca serves as an example of thoughtful urban design and demonstrates its dedication to both defense and the preservation of cultural heritage.

The city's well-preserved architecture, which includes structures like the Duomo di San Martino and the Guinigi Tower that are covered with oak trees representative of Lucca's medieval opulence, highlights its historical importance. The strategic significance of Lucca throughout the Roman Empire and its development under later rulers add to the city's rich historical tale.

The 16th and 17th-century city walls, which served as a beautiful promenade and represented Lucca's resistance to outside threats, are still completely in situ today. Visitors may get a look into a bygone age at this medieval fortress, which is a unique jewel. The musical heritage of Lucca gives its historical composition a distinctive touch. Giacomo Puccini was born in Lucca, a city that still has the sounds of opera and classical music. The annual Puccini Festival, held in an outdoor theater, highlights Lucca's vibrant cultural life and honors the composer's continuing legacy.

In addition, Lucca was crucial to the silk trade throughout the Renaissance, which boosted its wealth. The extravagant palaces and merchant mansions in the city, which represent the wealth created via trade routes, are clear signs of its economic history.

Let's sum up by saying that Lucca's historical importance is a mash-up of architectural wonders, strategic defenses, cultural legacies, and economic strength. Lucca is an intriguing place for anyone looking to immerse themselves in the annals of history since it encourages tourists to peel back the layers of its past as they meander through its cobblestone streets and medieval squares.

Walking the Walls

A trip through the centuries-old walls that capture the allure of this Tuscan treasure is walking the Walls in Lucca, which is like traveling through time. These Renaissance walls, which were constructed during the 16th and 17th centuries, are evidence of Lucca's long history and strategic importance.

The expansive views reveal a stunning patchwork of terracotta roofs, ancient towers, and the distant Apuan Alps as you walk along the wide, tree-lined promenade atop the walls. Under your feet, the city develops like a live novel, with each chapter recounted by the distinctive architectural features of the churches, palaces, and piazzas.

The walls themselves, once fearsome barriers, are now a peaceful haven. They allow residents and guests to enjoy a leisurely stroll or a quiet moment of introspection. They are lined with seats and shaded by old trees. Your trip is accompanied by the tranquil rustling of leaves and the sporadic ringing of distant church bells, creating a melodious symphony of the past and present.

Occasionally placed bastions break up the continuous wall and provide higher viewing vantage points. From these vantage points, you may go back in time to a time when the city was at risk from outside enemies and these walls served as a defense. The city is bathed in a warm light as the sun sets, and the city walls take on a beautiful quality. The cypress tree silhouettes that surround Lucca's sunset skyline transform it into an orange and pink-hued artwork. The emotional resonance that these physical buildings elicit—the tangible link between the past and the present that remains at each step of this historic journey—is what gives Walking the Walls in Lucca its ageless beauty.

Piazza dell'Anfiteatro

Lucca's Piazza dell'Anfiteatro is a stunning treasure that mirrors the city's lengthy history. Due to its distinctive elliptical form, this plaza serves as a reminder of Lucca's Roman history. It was once the location of a Roman amphitheater. This amphitheater's ruins have been cleverly transformed, and today medieval houses line the perimeter, resulting in a seamless fusion of architectural forms.

The lively atmosphere and seamless fusion of history and current life in the plaza are its main attractions. You may find beautiful cafés, bustling markets, and small stores hidden within the old buildings as you go along the Piazza dell'Anfiteatro. Each building is a chapter in a tale that details the development of the city. The circular design encourages a feeling of community as residents and guests congregate in the open area to take part in activities and festivals or to just take in the ever-present beauty of the surroundings.

The buildings' warm colors and floral and foliage decorations contribute to the magical atmosphere. A monument honoring Lucca-born musician Giacomo Puccini is located in the middle of the square. This detail highlights the city's cultural importance and artistic accomplishments.

Piazza dell'Anfiteatro is a live canvas where the past and present collide, not just a historical artifact. When you enter this plaza, it's like entering a doorway into Lucca's layers of history, where every stone has a tale to tell and every corner encourages you to take part in its continuous saga.

Cathedral of St. Martin

A magnificent Gothic masterpiece, the Cathedral of St. Martin, bears witness to centuries of outstanding architectural design and spiritual importance. Its tall spires, which are tucked away in the center of the city, pierce the sky and draw everyone's attention to it.

141

The cathedral was constructed over a number of centuries, starting in the 13th century and continuing through several eras, culminating in a beautiful fusion of architectural forms. Intricate stone sculptures that portray biblical themes and saints in minute detail decorate the cathedral's façade. The statues seem to come to life as the sun dances over its façade, silently narrating tales of faith and history. Grandiose wooden doors that protect the entry welcome both believers and others into this hallowed area where the past and present coexist.

One is instantly impressed by the cathedral's breathtaking interior upon entering. The nave is illuminated in an ethereal radiance by colossal stained glass windows that filter kaleidoscopic colors. The delicate columns that hold the vaulted ceilings' incredible heights seem to be reaching up to the skies. With altars, sculptures, and artifacts that capture the spiritual essence of bygone eras, each chapel in the cathedral is a haven of peace.

The magnificent organ, a symphony of pipes that fills the holy space with heavenly melody during religious events, is the cathedral's finest achievement. The air is filled with the echoes of songs and prayers, creating an ambience that is timeless.

In Summary to serve as a place of prayer, the Cathedral of St. Martin is now a tangible example of the continuing strength of human creativity and dedication. It continues to be a shining example of art, history, and religion, welcoming all who come to take part in the exquisite splendor of a holy journey through time.

Gothic and Romanesque Features

The lovely Italian city of Lucca, which combines Gothic and Romanesque architectural elements, offers a fascinating visual tour through many historical eras. The San Martino Cathedral, which is a famous example of Romanesque architecture, is located in the city. Its Romanesque architecture, which was popular from the 11th through the 13th century, is reflected in its strong walls, rounded arches, and beautiful arcading. In contrast, the Church of San Michele prominently displays Lucca's Gothic features. The Gothic architecture is evident in the pointed arches, ribbed vaults, and flying buttresses, which allude to a later time in the building process. This change in architectural style marks the passage from the substantial, fortified Romanesque buildings to the more complex and vertically oriented Gothic ones.

The city walls of Lucca, which were first constructed for protection during the Renaissance but also have older components, are an intriguing fusion of two styles. The strong Romanesque foundations serve as a solid platform, while subsequent embellishments like the pointed arches and merlons evoke the Gothic style. In addition to enclosing the city, these walls also include its architectural history, representing the layers of history that have influenced Lucca through the years.

In Summary, Lucca is a real example of how Gothic and Romanesque architectural elements may coexist. With each stride through its charming streets, travelers may travel through time as each architectural feature reveals a tale of its period.

Artistic Treasures Inside

An abundance of creative treasures are hidden behind the picturesque walls of Lucca, Italy, and call both aficionados and wanderers. The cultural legacy of Lucca is evidence of the city's lengthy history, and the city itself is home to a wide variety of creative marvels.

The façade of the Cathedral of San Martino is covered with elaborate sculptures that depict stories from earlier eras, making it a masterpiece. Enter the building to be enchanted by the spectacular mosaics that cover the flooring and Tintoretto's Last Supper, whose ethereal beauty tells biblical stories in a mosaic of hues.

Exploration is encouraged in the Palazzo Pfanner, a magnificent fusion of art and architecture. Its luxurious chambers are home to a variety of paintings and sculptures that demonstrate how creative trends have changed through time. Every chisel and stroke represents a different period in Lucca's aesthetic history.

Explore the winding lanes until you come upon the Church of San Frediano, with its golden mosaic façade shining like a prized treasure. Enter to discover the time-traveling, immersive heavenly paintings that grace the building's interiors. The aesthetic appeal of Lucca transcends conventional media. During the Lucca Biennale, modern artists from all over the globe transform the city's walls into a canvas by bringing the old stones to life with their cutting-edge inventions.

Overall, the Piazza dell'Anfiteatro becomes an outdoor gallery when dusk falls. Street entertainers and regional artists add to the atmosphere, weaving a vibrant tapestry of creativity that enthralls everyone who passes through.

Every cobblestone in Lucca appears to be whispering stories of creative genius, making it more than simply a city but a real-life masterpiece.

Guinigi Tower

The Guinigi Tower, a medieval jewelry that pierces the Tuscan skyline, serves as a timeless witness to Lucca's rich past. This architectural marvel, built in the 14th century by the wealthy Guinigi family, stands out for its distinctive rooftop garden, which represents affluence and a beautiful union of nature and human skill.

The tower's weathered stone stairs are a trip through time, with each creaky step carrying the echoes of a bygone past. As tourists ascend, a patchwork of terracotta roofs and historic buildings emerge from the city below. A lyrical reminder of Lucca's continuing attractiveness is provided by the panoramic perspective.

The Guinigi Tower's rooftop garden, a fantastical sanctuary perched above the medieval city, is its finest achievement. The city's scarlet roofs can be seen peeking through the lush vegetation, while shady holm oak trees tower above, their branches reaching for the sky. This lofty retreat provides not just solace but also a link to the Guinigi family's ideal of splendor. Given that it has survived both war and the test of time, the tower serves as a testament to Lucca's tenacity. It survived not only as a physical building but also as a library of tales inscribed on its stone walls. Each stone appears to be telling stories about lofty ideals, turbulent times in history, and the tranquil passing of endless days.

In conclusion, the Guinigi Tower, located in the heart of Tuscany, continues to be a beacon, luring travelers to marvel at its medieval magnificence and consider the complex relationship between history and architecture. It stands as a quiet watchman, a monument to the resilient character of a community that has elegantly accepted the past while embracing the future.

CHAPTER ELEVEN

Resources and Practical Information

Emergency Contact Numbers

It's important to be familiar with emergency phone numbers in Lucca, Italy. The following is a list of important numbers to have on hand:

1. Emergency Services (Carabinieri): In the event of any emergency, dial **112** for quick help. The Carabinieri can communicate with other agencies and respond to common crises.

2. Medical Emergency: Call **118** in the event of a medical emergency (ambulance). By dialing this number, you may reach emergency medical services and get helped right away.

3. Fire Department (Vigili del Fuoco): Dial **115** in the event of a fire. The Fire Department is prepared to handle both rescue and fire emergency situations.

4. Police (Polizia di Stato): Dial **113** if you need police help that is not related to a public emergency. This includes calling the police for assistance or reporting non-emergency situations.

5. Local Police (Polizia Municipale): The local police may help with concerns that aren't urgent, such as missing objects or traffic-related problems. Call them at **0583 4422** to get in touch.

6. Guardia Medical Services: Call **118** and ask for the Guardia Medica for medical advice for non-life-threatening medical conditions outside of regular business hours.

7. Poison Control Center (Centro Antiveleni): Dial **055 794 7815** to get in touch with the Poison Control Center in the event of poisoning. They provide advice on possible poisoning circumstances.

When contacting emergency lines, keep your cool, offer accurate information, and adhere to any directions that are given. Having these phone numbers handy will guarantee a prompt and efficient response in any circumstance.

Avoiding Scams and Tourist Traps

1. Research Accommodations: Before making a reservation, examine reviews on dependable sources to be sure you aren't falling for a badly run or dishonest hotel.

2. Street Sellers to Avoid: While some street sellers sell genuine products, be wary of anybody pressing you to make a purchase or advertising discounts that seem too good to be true since they often are.

3. Tourist Attraction Ticket Scams: To avoid falling for fake tickets or paying exorbitant rates from unlicensed dealers, get tickets for renowned attractions from authorized sources.

4. Taxi Scams: To avoid getting overcharged or taken on needless diversions, always utilize authorized taxi stands or reliable ride-sharing applications.

5. Fake Guided Tours: Before signing up for a guided tour, check the qualifications of the tour leaders and the company. Unauthorized guides could give you false information and harm your trip.

6. Check Restaurant Review: Check internet reviews of the restaurant you're thinking about to make sure it isn't a tourist trap with poor cuisine and exorbitant rates.

7. ATM Skimming Awareness: To lessen the chance that card skimming devices may be placed on less secure machines, use ATMs at respected banks, preferably within the bank.

153

8. Be Wary of "Helpful" Locals: While many locals are in fact kind, be wary if someone approaches you and offers you aid without your permission. It could serve as a decoy for pickpocketing or other fraud.

9. Verify Transportation Prices: To prevent getting overcharged by taxi drivers or private transportation services, check the price of transportation services in advance.

10. Keep Up With Local Scams: Stay informed on local scams to spot and prevent any new tricks that con artists may use.

You may reduce your chance of falling victim to rip-offs and tourist traps in Lucca by exercising caution and By following these guides, resulting in a more fulfilling and genuine vacation experience.

General Safety Precaution in Lucca

In Lucca, Italy, ensuring general safety is paramount for both residents and visitors. Various precautions contribute to a secure environment in this charming city.

1. Traffic Awareness: Lucca, with its narrow streets, encourages pedestrians and cyclists. Visitors should be mindful of traffic and use designated crossings.

2. Historical Site Caution: Lucca boasts historic architecture and landmarks. Visitors are urged to respect boundaries, avoid climbing on structures, and follow any posted guidelines to preserve the city's heritage.

4. Culinary Safety: Enjoying local cuisine is part of the Lucca experience. Travelers should be cautious about food allergies, verify the freshness of ingredients, and choose reputable establishments.

5. Weather Preparedness: Lucca experiences various weather conditions. Visitors should check forecasts and prepare accordingly, especially during hot summers or cooler winters.

6. Tourist Scam Awareness: Like any tourist destination, Lucca is not immune to scams. Travelers should be cautious of pickpockets, street vendors, and unsolicited services.

7. Emergency Services: Familiarize yourself with local emergency numbers and the location of medical facilities. Knowing these details can be crucial in case of unforeseen circumstances.

8. Public Transport Safety: Whether using buses or trains, adhering to safety guidelines on public transport is vital. Be aware of schedules, platforms, and maintain awareness of personal belongings.

9. Cultural Respect: Lucca has a rich cultural heritage. Visitors are encouraged to respect local customs, traditions, and quiet hours to ensure a harmonious coexistence with residents.

10. Environmental Responsibility: Lucca's beauty is also dependent on environmental stewardship. Dispose of waste properly, follow recycling guidelines, and contribute to the city's sustainability efforts.

11. Health Precautions: Stay informed about health advisories, carry necessary medications, and be aware of the nearest medical facilities. This is especially important for those with pre-existing health conditions.

By adhering to these general safety precautions, visitors can fully appreciate Lucca's charm while ensuring a secure and enjoyable stay.

Top Money saving Strategies for First- timer

1. Budgeting Fundamentals: Begin by creating a thorough budget that breaks down your income and spending. Sort your expenditure into categories to find places where you might make savings.

2. Emergency Fund: Create a safety net by setting aside three to six months' worth of living costs as an emergency fund. This reserve absorbs sudden financial shocks and keeps you from turning to borrowing in times of need.

3. Reduce Unnecessary Expenses: Consider your normal spending and find areas where you may make savings without compromising your standard of living. It can include cutting down on eating out, terminating unwanted subscriptions, or finding more affordable options.

4. Automatic Saving; Set up monthly automatic payments to your savings account to automate saving. You will always save money if you treat it as a non-negotiable expenditure.

5. Shop Smart: Shop wisely by mastering the skill of comparison shopping. Utilize coupons, look for deals, and think about purchasing generic products. Over time, little savings on commonplace purchases add up.

6. Debt Management Tip: Pay off high-interest bills first to prevent accruing more fees. Think about debt consolidation or negotiating better terms with creditors.

7. Invest Wisely: Invest wisely and early to take advantage of compound interest. To increase your returns, choose tax-advantaged funds like 401(k)s or IRAs.

8. Educate Yourself: Keep up with personal financial news. To make wise judgments, grasp the fundamentals of investment, get familiar with the many forms of insurance, and follow financial news.

9. Side Hustle: Look for ways to increase your income via a side business or freelance job. Your savings and debt repayment might be hastened by the additional income.

10. Mindful Spending: Practice thoughtful spending by considering if a purchase is necessary or just a wish. Delay gratification for non-essentials so you have time to consider their importance.

Keep in mind that achieving financial success is a journey, not a goal. You must be consistent and flexible as you manage the always shifting world of personal finance.

Wildlife and Nature Conservation

These are Lucca's distinctive wildlife and environmental conservation features:

1. Biodiversity Hotspot: Lucca is a hotspot for many different species because of its vast biodiversity. In order to support this vast range of flora and wildlife, conservation activities here concentrate on preserving and repairing ecosystems.

2. Protected Areas Several protected sites, including natural reserves and national parks, can be found in Lucca. These zones protect animals, ensuring that human activity doesn't alter their habitats.

3. Wildlife Rehabilitation: Conservation activities in Lucca place a strong emphasis on community engagement. Locals actively engage in projects and activities, which promotes a feeling of accountability and kinship with the environment.

4. Wildlife Rehabilitation Facilities: The city is home to facilities for the rescue and rehabilitation of sick, wounded, orphaned animals. These facilities are essential to the general well-being and adaptability of the local animal population.

5. Sustainable Tourism Practices: Lucca encourages eco-friendly tourist initiatives to lessen its negative effects on the environment. Eco-friendly lodging, considerate animal watching, and instruction on how guests may support conservation efforts are all included in this.

6. Reforestation Initiative: Lucca conducts reforestation activities to counteract deforestation because it understands the value of trees. This helps to mitigate climate change and conserve ecosystems while also capturing carbon.

7. Research and Monitoring: To get a better understanding of its ecosystems, the city funds scientific research and monitoring projects. This information serves as the foundation for knowledgeable conservation initiatives and flexible management techniques.

8. Education Initiatives: Schools and neighborhood groups are actively engaged in spreading the word about the value of protecting nature, with a particular emphasis on conservation education. This encourages the next generation to practice conservation.

9. Collaborations with NGOs: Lucca works with non-governmental organizations (NGOs) devoted to protecting animals and the environment. The conservation programs benefit from the added knowledge, resources, and spirit of cooperation that these collaborations provide.

10. Climate Resilience: Conservation activities in Lucca also focus on methods to improve the resilience of ecosystems in light of the effects of climate change. This involves actions to guarantee the long-term survival of animals and adapt to shifting climatic trends.

In order to protect its natural riches, Lucca has made a commitment to the protection of animals and the environment that is both comprehensive and community-driven.

Conclusion

A tapestry of memories that stick in the hearts of its visitors wraps up Lucca's travelog, a city engulfed in Renaissance splendor and historical importance. One can't help but feel deeply connected to the past as the sun sets over the city's medieval walls, throwing a warm light over cobblestone streets.

Piazza dell'Anfiteatro, a distinctive oval space that historically staged gladiatorial competitions, is where the tour's climax occurs. Today, it reverberates with the melodic sounds of street musicians and the laughter from bustling cafés. Visitors are completely surrounded by the wonderful fusion of historic buildings and modern culture. A panoramic perspective of the city's terracotta roofs and historical sites may be obtained by exploring Lucca's famous walls, a grand promenade lined with centuries-old trees. The guide recommends that visitors walk along this high road to fully see the city while also inhaling in the clean Tuscan air.

Trattorias and osterias in Lucca provide delicious treats. The book encourages readers to enjoy the straightforward flavors of regional cuisine, such as the famed Tuscan soup ribollita and delicate sweets like . Each taste becomes a sensory tour of the area's storied culinary history.

Visitors drawn to the Cathedral of San Martino are shown a vivid representation of Lucca's cultural strength by the complex façade and precious artworks stored inside. The tour reveals the creative story of the city and invites visitors to enjoy not only the destination but also the tales engraved in the building's structure and paintings. The gardens of Lucca, especially the Giardino Botanico, provide a peaceful haven for reflection. The book advises readers to stroll amid verdant vegetation while taking in the scents of blossoming flowers and the lingering echoes of the past.

The travel book makes a lasting impression by emphasizing the value of enjoying Lucca's leisurely pace in the last chapters. It exhorts visitors to abandon the haste of contemporary life and immerse themselves in this Italian treasure's leisurely pace.

In conclusion, the tour guide says goodbye knowing that all who enter Lucca's historic walls will carry memories of its attraction with them. Visitors leave with a piece of Lucca etched in their souls—a timeless memento from a city that whispers stories of bygone eras—whether they are enthralled by its history, charmed by its gastronomy, or affected by its art.

Printed in Great Britain
by Amazon